radical pairings

clementine e burnley

To Juliette

thanks so much for
coming out and
supporting poetry
and poets –
I hope you enjoy
these

warmly
Clementine

ignitionpress

Urvogel: the very first bird

for Kuva Likenyi

I'd like to think my line
began with a song,
"Elongi ye Musungedi".

In distant memory
perhaps a bugle sounds
before the charge across an ancient bridge

and a disorderly retreat.
Perhaps a dog laps
von Gravenreuth's blood

and the martyrs walk back to their farms.
No one's hanged, no one's forced
onto rock from fertile earth.

I'd like to think
someone drenches the soil
with palm wine.

I'd like to think of a choir,
and "Elongi ye Musungedi"
in contralto voice.

I went looking for America

When your very first hair piece
arrives by immigrant post
embrace its promise.

No butterfly cocoon—
more velvet moth's
soft dark drape
shaped into an asymmetrical bob.

Thank your daughter.
Say, *Ndutu.*
Wonderful-o.

Say, *I look like America-wanda.*
At night fit the lace front wig
to a smiling ebony skull stand.

Brush smooth the lines,
retire receding curls
under a satin night cap.

When you call, say
I met a man who calls himself a Black American.
He's never been to the U.S.A.

In his hair he keeps a metal Afro pick
with a Black Power fist
for its handle.

Don't say *I miss you.*
Don't say *I'm not always going to be around.*
Don't say *You're not coming home, are you?*

Portrait of an unnamed African girl, 1682

I have put on a ribbon tie choker
and for-best green satin to crouch beside
the Duchess of Portsmouth.
She's Louise de Kéroualle.
The painter's called Pierre Mignard. The scarlet coral
I hold sets off the Duchess's
gemstones, and her blue damask sleeve.
Her rich cascade of curls
contrasts with my shaven head.
My corner of the canvas is lost to shadow.
The artist paints even my fingernails deep brown.
Gloom lifts around the Duchess.
I know my own name. I've held
this smile for so long that my teeth feel dry.
Her look's neutral. My work's to rest a tender
gaze on Louise de Kéroualle's face.
Hers is to sit still on a golden stool.
Pierre Mignard places the Duchess's hand
on my back. My neck's locked. Her leg muscles twitch.

The Origins of Birds

for Joseph Ebakisé Burnley

Few songbirds survive their test flight.
A bar-tailed godwit may journey
twelve thousand kilometres to nest.
The first migration serves
to build an internal map
from remembered scents, and star charts.
Night-time summons Polaris.
A sun compass,
quantum effects, the short-lived pairings
of molecules in eyes
helps voyagers chart magnetic field lines.

Roof slates are lines of weakness
faults in the morning.
Blackbirds
still overlook the path
between Colwyn Bay and Rhos-on-Sea.
Holes in the sand are a cat perhaps.
The caress of darker hands on pale forearms
still sparks uproar.
Boys with skin the brown of earth,
still walk this coast
and recall another shore
where manatees range.

Abia is an ancient presence in the Rio del Rey.
A male crop in the clearing.
A root of tapering length.
Abia interrupts the forest
after the rich soil dams early rains
and weeds throng the new season's sprouts.
In the dry heat, winged tendrils scramble a wooden trellis.
Brown skinned tubers swell unseen.
Abia is frost-tender foliage
that yellows in late November.
Abia is our harvests' pale flesh.

My cousin after many rounds of chemotherapy

says *having cancer is like a full-time job*
she's always paid her taxes
claimed no benefits
committed no felonies
studied for degrees
on the phone she recites
her four different types of drugs
two mastectomies
and twenty-seven lymph nodes
she can't leave her country
and I can't leave mine
we approach each other in each call
although it's her PICC line
her Uber rides
and her amazing nurses
she shares her jokes
her MRI team selfies
her clinical trial
her drug-induced headache
the morning she spent in the garden
gorging herself on early sun
and later she shares her hospital awards
it's her three-hour muzak playlist
on the phone to immigration
her shoulders heaving
her wry face
her laughter at the news
she *need not concern herself*
her leave to remain
can be awarded posthumously

Berber for water

for N'déyé Mareame Sarr

You can see Africa
from the high Alpujarra, they say.
Go now.

Here is Albussarat
suspended on the southern edge
of the Sierra Nevada.

Pack cucumbers, sheep's milk
cheese and a Conference pear.
From the winding road look for the glint

of a thousand polytunnels.
Here were zereshk.
Here was sumac.

Go further, for there nothing grows.
Walk to where the call to prayer
echoed through the woods.

Slow where trees hesitate.
Stone grooves yawned here.
This way lies a dried-up sluice.

Snowmelt spills swift
without a network of levees
buried to ward off droughts.

Here is the last tree greening at the heart
of a hollowed-out coppice.
Here is the last meal.

All the way, underfoot,
are silted-up veins.
Everywhere absence dwells.

Old Crow talks to a Ghost Boy

for George Steane

It hurts to think of you buried there, I say
to George. *The unmarked grave.*

Onyx eyes rivet me where I lie, my feathers pressed
roadkill flat,

the tarmac still warm from the afternoon's sun.
George listens more thoughtfully than I expect.

This sky seems wrong, he says. Around us, air vortices
swirl from delivery trucks. He must shout above the noise.

After the shipwreck, the racist gun. The cold circle of muzzle
pressed to his temple urged him to stay on the listing deck.

After the lifeboat's miraculous return
another long voyage to Colwyn Bay.

George died years later, of a chill.
It seems anticlimactic, he says.

The moonlight bruises his skin.
His feet are the blue of crushed horseshoe crabs.

Tell me what colour this is, he says, gesturing at the sky.
Lapis lazuli, I say, shy. It's a fancy word.

Earthrise paints his soles indigo.
He undoes a suture in the night.

Concentric circles swell around us.
He is a stillness at the heart.

a night-migrating songbird navigates great distances alone

my mother is never on time
she's in perfect time.
for who else would an airplane or a PTA board wait?

her magics are as hard to predict as the fall
of atoms decaying in a closed box.
when she looks at the rotary phone, it rings.
she gifts me her crooked middle toe,

she can sense direction
by the fall of photons,
filter microplastics from breast milk.
when mortuary shelves

become the ledger of a small town
she repairs hydroelectric plants.
as we arbitrate her funeral on Zoom
rolling blackouts abate.

the women of her line scoff at recipes
measure out ingredients by eye and heft
find secrets best stored in their heads.
there's an echo of my mother

in the way my small talk turns awkward.
things I ponder upon:
how electrosmog can disrupt a robin's magnetic compass?
why pink bats return to unliveable shores?

when I make her ginger beer
it's as fiery as I recall.
if time is circular
I can surprise her in Piazza San Marco.

I like her.
she wears a striped sepia baby doll dress.
she's not my mother then.

La Peregrina: a wandering pearl

Not wanting to feel
made me.
I owe my near-perfect symmetry to
a rotational force of 0.1 Newtons—
the weight of a strawberry.

I'm required to shine
like the creatures I adorn.
I don't bleed.

My ripples are organised in parallel
like the lines of longitude on a globe.
The voids in my veins snare light waves.

I have survived the journey
from fleshy roots to iridescent pendulum.
I make common cause with anything soft.

I rested near Cubagua and Margarita
between the tenacious barques of
conquistadors and the seabed.

My first owner was addicted
to the umami of damaged objects.

I fled the Crown in 1560.
Someone saw me yellowing
alone in Panama.

I gave the enslaved worker
who took me prisoner in Seville, his liberty.
He hid me in his mouth.

Wayfarers

I cross the border at dawn,
riding high at the front of a Luton van.

Cars circle roundabouts the right way,
this country greets me aslant.

Since English manners shut my mouth
I don't ask why
the moving company's called Kingdom.

I don't ask where God was an hour ago,
in the No Man's Land of Calais.

I say *brother* as I say *feather,*
some words carry more weight than others.

While I slept, he coiled his spine,
into the shape of a dream.

While we drove, he held on. This country greets him
with surprise. *He's alive. How's he not burned?*

I have reversed over a mirror,
unknowing. I have said *in the end*
we all bleed the same.

Now he squats by the axle.
Why am I nervous for myself, when this island welcomes
the papers I carry?

This island welcomes the man I drive beside.
My hair grows upwards.
His veins reflect blue light.

Wolf

though our ancestors hunted her kind
through highland rainforests
ten thousand years ago.
though nettles grow up over hill scars,
through a stand of dock
she watches, curious.
boys lay a perimeter of piss around a canvas tent.
triangled ears turn
to the sounds
of their small, safe deaths
their tenderness.
a wolf is spotted aboard a train in Brussels.
in pubs, on the Polish-German border
instead of musk deer
staghorn ferns are nailed to wooden trophy boards.
she leaves a boggy stink in stairwells near Glasgow Green.
the treads never wash clean of her.
watchfires linger
after three pregnant wolves are shot on the way to France.
near the Forest of Dean, a dog walker raises the alarm.
when night blots out the purple of pennyroyal
the search for wolves is abandoned
among brambles so thick
a pizza box is a smudge in the surveillance footage.
the DNA profile captured in her scat
is tagged, *lone female.*
she leaves a paw print between the daylilies.
the shadow of an overhead power line marks her flank.

your name is "a god has returned"

for David Oluwale

a person cradles you
a person holds you up to the rainwater
from the galvanized roof

a person babas you on her back
the woman of the house
fries small white fish

a person named you Oluwale
you were raised in the quarters
you rolled sand grains into ant lion wells
you looked for work

the watchmen yawned
bones stiff after the shift
rich people's dreams require a nightly vigil
and you like to have a good time

sometimes your head scatters
or you find work or you find none
another night in the door mouth

for true
there is no work
when you call all the lines ring busy.

Matryoshka: Russian dolls

When a mother's body unzips, there's a parliament inside
where great-grandmothers and grandmothers convene.
A child can take its mother home. They say,
to live in a body is to submit to its laws.

Great-grandmothers and grandmothers convene.
A mother pinches the wound shut. They say,
to live in a body is to submit to its laws.
Don't pray for children when you only want a daughter or a son.

A mother pinches the wound shut.
A mother's body is a hometown. They say,
don't pray for children when you only want a daughter
or a son. Don't pass on the last names of men.

A mother's body is a hometown where
Bible bashers and palm-wine drinkers walk the streets.
When a mother's body unzips, there's a parliament inside,
they say. *A child takes its mother home.*

Janus on pill box Sunday

The woman I meet in the toilet has her church clothes on. She had an en suite bathroom with bidet. The woman had children, many of them. What were their names…? the woman asks.

She counts pills; one big round and grey, two small, one long, one with a line through the middle and one with a cross. She is good at taking pills, she says.

She starts to laugh but her mouth is full of water. I am afraid, dry choke a small one with no cross. She doesn't know what the pills do. The woman laughs till both our faces blur with tears.

Thaw

Inside, a hundred doors fly open.
Inside me generations
pocket one-way tickets,
ride in caravans,
stride across tundra,
step off trains,
scramble across barricades.
Their small boats greet the tide.
Roots spread,
the origin of many British plants is uncertain.
At eight in the evening
hoofbeats take the road
and the traffic in Glen Etive shrinks back.
Bridges are pen strokes through mist,
glassy lochs, grey call of night-time heron,
the riot of packing, unpacking,
cities changing—
for years I have kissed snakes,
scaled ladders,
fumbled over place settings.
The interview panels are always white.
People and cars go back and forth,
in the end
islands dissolve.

Broken English

She carries a letter in my grandmother's
copperplate script.

She has a big voice for a small person,
this early-rising, suitcase-trading,

Blood-of-Jesus old woman who's taken my bed.
Her eyes are the dark blue of magpies.

Her eyes are the grey stars
of approaching blindness.

I can say *Kana jin harshen turanci*
kuwa? in a faithful accent.

I can say *Na gode*
both hands outstretched.

I do not know
how to say *English*.

She must have her reasons—all the motley colours
of words from seven languages.

Her speech interrupts an empire
without a single shot.

Homecoming

my father plants moonflowers, my father plants green mangos above the silver rise and fall of his aluminium roof. green snakes come to live in the branches, mosquitos suspend their eggs in yesterday's floods, and dark moths come to night-scented blooms, bats slam so boisterous into one another that overripe fruit smears the air, and my father grumbles. when coconuts dent the ceiling boards above my father's head, he threatens to fell the trees he planted just so he can sleep. my father's bedroom is quiet when I return. he is between bark and pith, where bat wings fold the day closed.

How to eat frogs

Grandmothers croak welcome.
Crows watch from a sagging power line
while I unpack the bulky suitcase.

Grandmothers test me with my sisters
engaged to marry sons of the soil.

Grandmothers think my nose ring is for free girls,
ask: Did you swallow cloven hoofs or horse meat?
So why do you rob our peace?

Do your shoulders move one by one
when you dance the mbwaya?

Who fed you eggs before you were two?
Who named you swallow?

Where is your umbilical buried?
What kénékéné thing ate your tongue?

In the market, between purple pyramids of
piled up tomatoes, orange culubar, and bush plums

Grandmothers ask: how many home boys
has your any-kind careless talk mouth thrown away?

The cool palm is benediction to my forehead before
Grandmothers squat at the fireplace,

muttering: If you're going to cook a white frog, choose a fat one—
If you're going to eat snails, don't expect to win
a hundred metre dash.

I'm asking my grandmothers if
we were too much, too soon
too loud, too young?

We all need sweetness, they reply, but
would you rather be a meal or a snack?

My grandmothers ask:
If you give the milk away for free
who's going to buy the cow?

Protectorates

for Rudolphe Douala Manga Bell

Daughter countries are posed on a map
their borders ruler-straight.

A native tongue is in a mother's gift.
One sense of the word "gift" in German

is contagion. In the aftermath of empires
language is a broken promise—

the past, a looted house
where the gate hangs loose.

Beneath crowded trees, apples rot.
And yet, below the graft lines

new growth lurches,
scion wood flourishes.

How to wipe clean the axe
after the edge cuts through?

Some branches are reverting to type.
After slash burning, a host of coppice shoots

rallies from the trunks. The unsung
is always trying to have the last word.

Notes

The radical-pair hypothesis centres on the mechanism by which water soluble proteins, known as cryptochromes, in the retinas of migratory songbirds may help them detect the direction of the Earth's magnetic field.

> The quantum nature of the radical-pair hypothesis has attracted the interest of theoreticians. [...] One of the main reasons for all this attention is that the two electron spins in a singlet radical pair are entangled. Entanglement (a quantum phenomenon famously described by Einstein as "spooky action at a distance") in the context of a radical pair means that the behavior of one electron spin is affected by what happens to the other even though they may be well separated and have a negligible interaction energy.
>
> [...] Current evidence strongly suggests that night-migratory songbirds have a light-dependent, magnetic-compass sensor located in their eyes and that the underlying mechanism relies on the quantum spin dynamics of photoinduced radical pairs probably generated in cryptochromes.
>
> 'The Radical-Pair Mechanism of Magnetoreception' by P. J. Hore and Henrik Mouritsen, *Annual Review of Biophysics*, Vol. 45: 299–344, 2016.

Urvogel or Archaeopteryx is a black feathered birdlike dinosaur, thought to be one of the oldest known fossil birds. It lived 150 million years ago. Archaeopteryx remains were found in Bavaria, Southern Germany in 1861.

Karl Freidrich Freiherr von Gravenreuth was a Bavarian German colonial army officer. He was ambushed and killed by Kpé fighters —led by Chief Kuva Likenyi, in the Battle of Buea, Southwest Region of Cameroon on November 5, 1891.

La Peregrina is a named pearl that was once in the Spanish Crown Jewels. The lines in italics are from an article on *BBC Future*. The poem began in a workshop with Fred D'Aguiar and Sarah Howe, as part of the TIDE research project.

'Portrait of an unnamed African girl, 1682' is a response to "Louise de Kéroualle, Duchess of Portsmouth with an unknown female attendant" by Pierre Mignard, 1682. It came to life in the same TIDE research project workshop mentioned above.

'Abia' is the Efik Ibiobio word for yam. In the Southeastern Nigerian and Cameroonian Ibiobio cultural tradition, yams were mainly grown by men.

Matryoshka are sets of wooden dolls, of decreasing sizes, which can be placed so they nest inside each other.

'Na gode' is Hausa for 'Thank you.'

'Kana jin harshen turanci kuwa?' is Hausa for 'Do you speak English?'

Acknowledgements

Many thanks to the editors of the following publications in which versions of these poems have appeared: *Magma*, *The Poetry Review*, *Anthropocene*, *The Selkie*, *Oluwale Now!* and *Before Them, We*.

Thank you to Hugh McMillan for choosing 'How to eat frogs' for the Scottish Poetry Library's Best Scottish Poems 2021; to the judges of the Oluwale Competition 2022 for shortlisting a version of 'your name is "a god has returned"'; to Liz Chege and Siana Bangura for their support during the Scottish Poetry Library commission for the Imaginarium strand of the Africa in Motion Festival 2021; and to Bernardine Evaristo for the 2021 Sky Arts RSL Writers Award (Non-Fiction).

These poems would not exist without the mentorship of Hannah Lavery, Nick Makoha, Colin Grant and Chimamanda Ngozi Adichie.

My gratitude also goes out to Dean Atta, Jess Brough, Jeda Lewis, Andrés N. Ordorica, Alycia Pirmohamed and Titilayo Farukuoye at the Scottish BPOC Writers Network.

I appreciate the guidance provided by Malika Booker, Roger Robinson, Raymond Antrobus and Dante Micheaux during the Obsidian Foundation 2020 retreat. Thank you to Suzanne Alleyne for "just-in-time" support.

Thank you to my peers in Sharon Dodua Otoo's *Witnessed* writing project, the 2018 Purple Hibiscus Writers group, Obsidian 2020 Group 'B' poets, the Curtis Brown Fiction Writers group, the Moniack Mhor 2022 Memoir Writers group and Cath Drake's poetry feedback group.

Zakia, Larissa, Jaya, Sarah, Adiza, Christina, Pey, Emma, Kim, Selali, Dom, Memuna, Remi, Fran, Tash, Chelsea, Calah, Basil, thank you for the deep talks and belly laughs.

Thank you to everyone at **ignition**press for believing in my project and for giving my poems a permanent home in print. Thank you to Claire Cox for guiding this work into the world with such rigour, warmth and humour.

Much love to Rea, Zoe and Noa for encouraging me to grapple with what troubles us all. Thanks are due: to Iain, for waiting. To my aunts who are like mothers and to my cousins who are like siblings. To my siblings, for listening. To my parents for their generosity, grace and for their dance moves. To Catherine, who never wavered. To Uncle Alhaji Daihirou for encouraging me to return. To Alice Etondi Daihirou-Martin for the books, and your love of reading. To my sister Anne, who knows.

MIX
Paper from responsible sources
FSC® C007326
www.fsc.org

Oxford Brookes is committed to the environment.
This document is printed using processes that are:

100% Net Carbon Negative
100% Renewable Energy
100% ISO14001
100% eco-friendly simitri® toner
100% Recyclable Stock

Zero % waste to landfill

Printed by seacourt – proud to be counted amongst the top environmental printers in the world